P9-DCM-225

1000 FEELINGS FOR WHICH THERE ARE NO NAMES

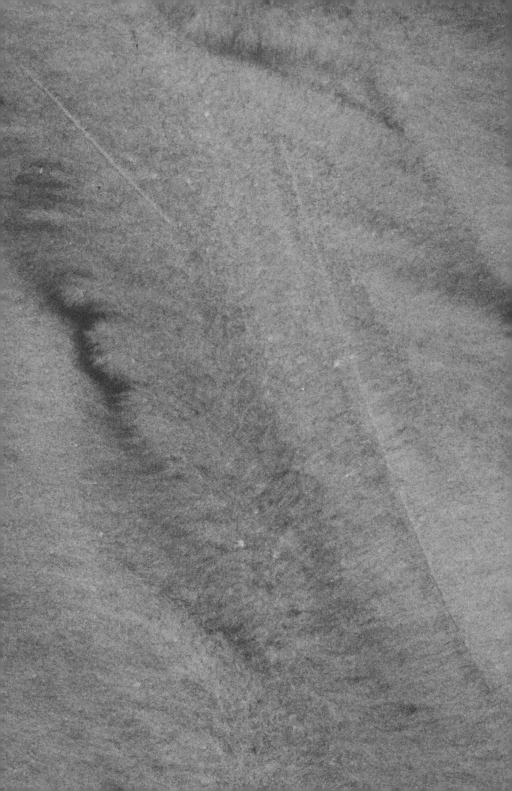

1000 FEELINGS FOR WHICH THERE ARE NO NAMES

MARIO GIORDANO

TRANSLATED BY ISABEL FARGO COLE

ILLUSTRATED BY RAY FENWICK

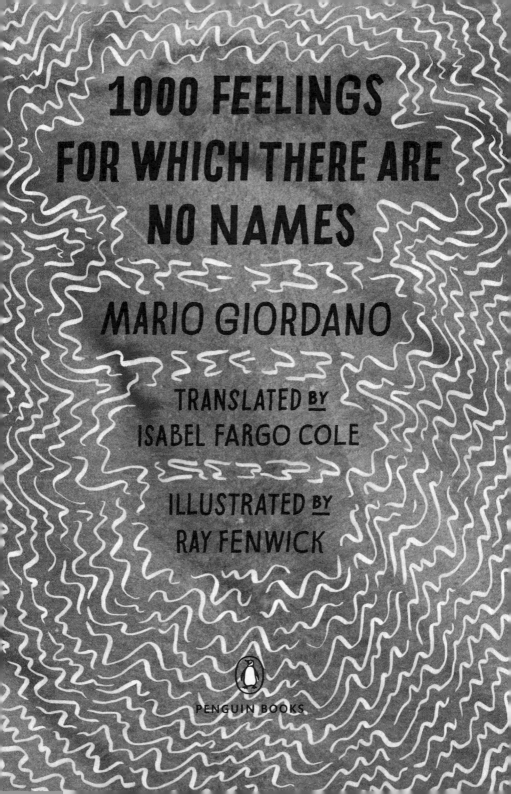

PENGUIN BOOKS

PENGUIN BOOKS

Published by the Penguin Group
Penguin Group (USA) LLC
375 Hudson Street
New York, New York 10014

USA | Canada | UK | Ireland | Australia | New Zealand | India | South Africa | China
penguin.com
A Penguin Random House Company

First published in Penguin Books 2014

Copyright © 2013 by Berlin Verlag in der Piper Verlag GmbH, Munchen
Translation copyright © 2014 by Isabel Fargo Cole
Penguin supports copyright. Copyright fuels creativity, encourages diverse voices, promotes free
speech, and creates a vibrant culture. Thank you for buying an authorized edition of this book
and for complying with copyright laws by not reproducing, scanning, or distributing any part of it
in any form without permission. You are supporting writers and allowing Penguin to continue to
publish books for every reader.

Originally published in German as *1000 Gefuhle fur die es keinen namen gibt* by Piper Verlag,
Munich.

ISBN 978-0-14-312528-0

Printed in the United States of America

1   3   5   7   9   10   8   6   4   2

Designed by Ray Fenwick

SOME
SUGGESTIONS
FOR USE
(BY WAY OF A PREFACE)

For home and travel use.
Flip through. And find feelings.
(Don't forget the index.)
Remember.
Combine feelings in new ways.
Pick a number between one
and one thousand.
Look things up.
Use as your daily oracle.
Draw up a Top Ten list of your
favorite feelings.
Make some up yourself.
Write them down at once.
(Before they get away!)
Share feelings with others.

MARIO GIORDANO
(FEELING #310)
OCTOBER 2012

1000 FEELINGS FOR WHICH THERE ARE NO NAMES

1

The exhilaration
at the first glimpse
of the sea.

2

The fear
of speaking
in public.

3

The

that she likes
the present.

4

THE

SHAME AT YOUR OWN

SCHADENFREUDE.

5
THE _ENVY_ OF OTHER PEOPLE'S SNAPPY COMEBACKS.

6
The READY-FOR-ACTION FEELING
after getting a new haircut.

7
The
snug feeling
when you're sick in bed and everyone feels sorry for you and waits on you hand and foot.

8
The _remorse_ over a trivial act of thoughtlessness.

9

The helpless feeling
when funny games are played
at bridal showers.

10

The delight
at finding new
friends.

11

The
pleasure of giving
a present.

12

THE MOUNTING RAGE
WHEN YOU WANT TO TALK AND
HE JUST CLAMS UP.

13

THE SHOCK
AT YOURSELF FOR WISHING
DEATH UPON SPEEDERS.

14

The profound _confidence_
that you descend from Adam & Eve,
not from the apes.

15

The _relief_ when
no one picks up
the phone.

16

The _jealousy_ of
your life partner's
blissful sleep.

17

The _anxiety_ when they
check tickets, even though
yours is valid.

18

**THE _DREAD_
OF ICEBREAKER
GAMES.**

19

The
stupefaction at a truly
brazen excuse.

20

THE
CHILDISH JOY
AT THE
FIRST
SNOW.

21

The delight
at your guests'
hearty appetites.

22

THE SHAME
OF GETTING CAUGHT
RED-HANDED.

23

THE DISAPPOINTMENT WHEN BAD NEWS YOU'RE BRACED FOR FAILS TO MATERIALIZE.

24

THE FEAR THAT IT'LL STILL LEAVE A BITTER AFTERTASTE.

25

The

in your playlist.

26

The anger at your inability to get angry.

27

*The thrill at
the awesome sound of the
eight-cylinder motor.*

28

THE AMAZEMENT AT
HOW FAR SOME PEOPLE COME WITH
SO LITTLE TALENT.

29

THE SHAME AT
HOW FAR YOU'VE COME WITH
SO LITTLE TALENT.

30

The

after a properly
spicy curry.

31
The pity
for a
broken toy.

32
The mounting fury
when trying to untangle a
snarled necklace.

33
THE PRIDE
AT HITTING ON THE
MAGIC WORD.

34
THE WORRY
THAT YOU WON'T HAVE
ENOUGH GAS.

35
The delight
at having warm feet
in the summer.

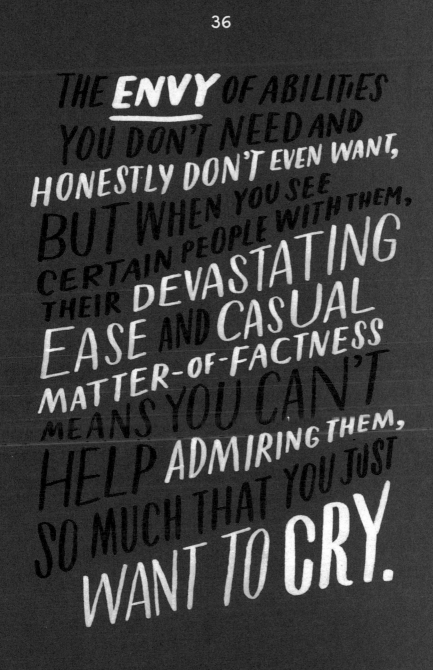

THE **ENVY** OF ABILITIES YOU DON'T NEED AND HONESTLY DON'T EVEN WANT, BUT WHEN YOU SEE CERTAIN PEOPLE WITH THEM, THEIR DEVASTATING EASE AND CASUAL MATTER-OF-FACTNESS MEANS YOU CAN'T HELP ADMIRING THEM, SO MUCH THAT YOU JUST WANT TO **CRY.**

37

The <u>embarrassment</u> when you're caught picking your nose.

38

The <u>fear</u> of small furry animals.

39

The <u>joy</u> of horsing around with your own wife.

40

THE PANIC AS TAX DAY APPROACHES.

41

The <u>bashfulness</u> that follows a compliment.

42

The

YEARNING

for adventures in
faraway countries.

43

THE PRIDE IN
HAVING STOOD ATOP THE
BERLIN WALL IN 1989.

44

The worry
that you might be stuck
in the matrix.

45

The fear of
MONSTERS
under the bed.

46

*The fear of
taking part in other people's
religious rituals.*

47

The fear that the
neighbor's monitor lizard might
sneak in over the balcony.

48

THE FEAR THAT *FURRENERS*
WILL BE COMING TO TAKE AWAY OUR JOBS
AND OUR WOMEN.

49

THE FEAR OF
TOTALLY MISSING OUT ON LIFE IF
THINGS GO ON LIKE THIS.

50

The warm feeling when your
friends throw you an unexpected
farewell party before your trip.

51

The _vexation_ when
you're packing and realize the
bag won't hold everything.

52

The
sadistic pleasure of
swatting a fly.

53

The _dread_ of the deep dark hole
you're going to fall down if something
doesn't happen soon.

54

The _relief_
at an outrageous
stroke of luck.

55

The _dismay_ of
realizing how much you're
like your father.

56

The g<u>lee</u> when you sang your own praises for once, and everyone nodded in agreement.

57

The <u>disillusionment</u> of not belonging to someone's intimate circle after all.

58

THE <u>IMPOTENCE</u> OF BEING TOTALLY UNABLE TO HELP HER WITH THIS PROBLEM.

59

The <u>rage</u> when yet again you were too shy to complain about the poor service.

60

The <u>fear</u> that someone will discover your failure to perform an assigned task.

61

The gratification
when you realize this really
was the right decision.

62

The ambition to get everything
just a little bit cheaper.
Preferably free.

63

THE LONGING TO HURL
YOURSELF TO THE FLOOR LIKE A CHILD
AND START SCREAMING.

64

The horror of
waking up one morning
and finding yourself
married
to the nasty neighbor
from across the hall.

66

The _envy_ of people
who can give a speech
off the cuff.

67

The _doubt_ whether
this spontaneous date was
really such a good idea.

68

The **wistful knowledge**
that this moment will
never return.

69

The _pride_
of having a cz or sz
in your name.

70

The _infuriation_ of
having a solo and missing
your entrance.

71

The **anticipation** of
your family's return
from vacation.

72

The **enjoyment** of
popping the bubbles in
the bubble wrap.

73

THE **DREAD**
OF CATCHING THE FLU
ON THE SUBWAY.

74

The affection
for your partner's
love handles.

75

THE **ANNOYANCE** AT MISSING
AN OPPORTUNITY THAT YOU WON'T
GET AGAIN ANYTIME SOON.

76
THE **PRIDE** AT GETTING SO MANY LIKES ON THE CAT PHOTO YOU JUST POSTED.

77
THE **IMPATIENCE** AT HAVING TO LISTEN TO SOMEONE BLATHER ON AND ON.

78
The

of opening your mouth at the dentist's.

79
The **delight** when a baby grabs your finger and won't let go.

80

*The _hope_ of getting
an indecent proposal
like in the movie.*

81

The **embarrassment**
of admitting you're
a country fan.

82

*The **impotent rage** at that
nasty sliding tackle against
our center forward.*

83

THE GRATITUDE
AT NOT KNOWING
WAR.

84

The
pleasure of going over
the shopping list.

85

THE <u>JEALOUSY</u> THAT YOU CAN'T JOIN IN THE GOSSIPING.

86

THE <u>HOPE</u> THAT FOR ONCE IT'LL BE HOT ENOUGH TO GET OFF SCHOOL.

87

The <u>enjoyment</u> of your daydreams.

88

The <u>nostalgia</u> for butterflies in your stomach.

89

The <u>anger</u> at the early-morning birds.

90
THE HAPPINESS
OF FINDING THE RIGHT
HAIRDRESSER.

91
The gratification
when people think you're
younger than you are.

92
The gratification
when people think you're
older than you are.

93
The wrath when not a single
damn person reacts to your
indignant letter of complaint.

94
The
world-weariness of
an eight-year-old.

95

The _serenity_ of having nothing more to prove.

96

The <u>chagrin</u> when you're caught at a minor insurance swindle.

97

THE BLISSFUL <u>ABSENTMIND</u>
-<u>EDNESS</u> OF DRAGGING YOUR FEET AS YOU WALK.

98

THE <u>COWARDICE</u> THAT WON'T LET YOU TELL HIM THE TRUTH TO HIS FACE.

99

The <u>pride</u> at making her laugh.

100

The felicity
of the
first touch.

101

The infinite disappointment when the D.J. puts on the last dance at 5:00 A.M.

102

THE AWE OF GLIMPSING THE HIMALAYAS FROM THE PLANE.

103

THE EMBARRASSMENT OVER THE COFFEE STAIN ON YOUR TROUSERS.

104

THE MOUNTING DESPERATION WHEN FACING THE EMPTY PAGE.

105

THE ASTONISHMENT
AT BEING LOVED
UNCONDITIONALLY.

106

*The shame at
being incapable of it
yourself.*

107

The anxiety that maybe you're
not a real man because you've
never been to a brothel.

108

*The even greater
anxiety at the idea of going
to a brothel.*

109

The happiness of sitting
together at the window
and simply looking out.

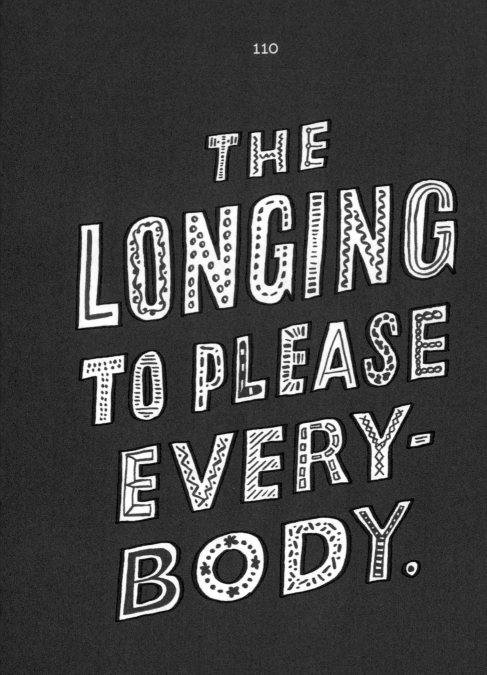

THE LONGING TO PLEASE EVERY-BODY.

111

*The <u>rage</u> at slowpokes
in the middle lane
of the highway.*

112

The

that the water you're swimming
in is full of little bugs that will lay
their eggs under your skin.

113

*THE <u>RELIEF</u>
AT BEING OVER
SIX FEET TALL.*

114

*The <u>misgiving</u>
that something's
not right.*

115

The

*of not living up to
her standards.*

116

THE PRIDE
IN YOUR SORE MUSCLES
AFTER THE HIKE.

117

The happiness when your
friends rejoice ungrudgingly
along with you.

118

THE DISCOMFORT AT
UNDRESSING IN FRONT OF THE
DOCTOR'S ASSISTANT.

119

The disappointment
when you didn't get
caught after all.

120

The envy
of attractive
feet.

121

THE FEAR
OF A CHINESE
INVASION.

122

THE GRATITUDE OF
SHARING SOMEONE'S UMBRELLA
IN THE POURING RAIN.

123

The
relief after the
knuckle cracks.

124

The <u>loneliness</u>
following
the farewell.

125

The feisty

felt toward men who ruthlessly
stuff their excessively heavy carry-on
luggage into the overhead rack.

126

THE
<u>EUPHORIA</u> AFTER
A VICTORY.

127

The <u>misgiving</u> that the
Catholic Church might turn out to be
right about everything after all.

128

*The <u>delight</u> at the
soft hum of colorful little
pinwheels in the garden.*

129

THE <u>CRAVING</u>
FOR A
FLEETING TOUCH.

130

The

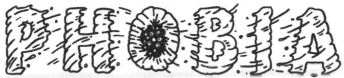

that the Large Hadron Collider
near Geneva will create a black
hole that will swallow us all.

131

The <u>pride</u> when
you're meeting up with
New Yorkers in New York.

132
THE CONTRITION OVER
THE FACT THAT OLD PEOPLE
DISGUST YOU.

133
The disappointment
when checking your
voice mail.

134
The pleasure
of uninhibited
trash talk.

135
The sorrow
that you can never be
a child again.

136
The relief that
you'll never have to be
a child again.

137

The <u>shock</u> of
meeting someone who
looks just like you.

138

The joy at the trustfulness of your pony, the first time it unhesitatingly follows you through a puddle.

139

THE <u>PRIDE</u> WHEN YOU
FINALLY GET TO SIT IN THE FRONT
SEAT NEXT TO DAD.

140

The
~~agony~~ ~~agony~~
~~agony~~ ~~AGONY~~ ~~AGONY~~
~~agony~~ ~~agony~~ ~~AGONY~~
~~AGONY~~ ~~AGONY~~ ~~AGONY~~
<u>ag</u>ony of choice.

141

The pride
in your own
ambition.

142

The unshakeable
assurance of the
tour guide.

143

THE INCREDULITY
AT OTHER PEOPLE'S
BAD TASTE.

144

The relief
that follows the
confession.

145

The dismay, at the first class
reunion in thirty years, that nothing
has changed for the better.

146

The fury
at his managing to
stay so calm.

147

The **fear** that she'll
totally lose it
if that guy says,

WE DON'T HAVE THAT
IN STOCK RIGHT NOW

One more time.

148

The desire to touch him.
Right now.
Just because.

149

THE TRIUMPH AT
SHOWING YOUR INNER COUCH POTATO
WHO'S BOSS.

150

The panic that this fight might never end.

151

The strange RESTLESSNESS at the sight of college girls on summer break.

152

THE EUPHORIA OF EMERGING FROM ICE-COLD WATER.

153

The longing to dissolve into thin air.

154

The

that you might have to use the
defibrillator in the hall one day.

155

The <u>relief</u>
of having put it
behind you.

156

The <u>anxiety</u>
of still having it to
look forward to.

157

The tender <u>delight</u>
at sharing a term of
endearment.

158

The <u>rancor</u> when someone points out the little *tics* you wish you had under control—but don't.

159

The *panic* at the sight of the ski slope.

160

The  **JOY** of feeling you're alive.

161

The <u>fear</u> of the next flare-up.

DISCOMBOBULATION.

163

The <u>sudden</u> <u>resolve</u> to follow the woman up there in the red Mini Cooper and just see what happens.

164

The

♂♀EMBARRASSMENT

when the cleaning lady barges into the airport restroom and starts mopping as if you weren't there.

165

The <u>helplessness</u> of having to comfort a total stranger.

166

The <u>jealousy</u> of friends who are vacationing in your favorite spot.

167
THE <u>EMBARRASSMENT</u>
OF RUNNING STRAIGHT INTO
A GLASS DOOR.

168
The joyful <u>anticipation</u> of a surprised face.

169
THE <u>PRIDE</u>
OF BEING ASKED
FOR ADVICE.

170
The <u>fear</u> of not having done enough.

171
The <u>anger</u> at your coworker's insensitivity.

172

The _anxiety_ that
everyone can smell your
sweaty armpits.

173

The _worry_ that the
cash machine won't give
back your card.

174

The _embarrassment_
when you realize you're
talking to yourself.

175

THE _SURPRISE_ AT HOW
TENACIOUS YOU CAN BE WHEN
PUSH COMES TO SHOVE.

176

The _disappointment_
of finding out how weak
grown-ups really are.

177

The <u>delight</u>
in your partner's
quirks.

178

The
MISCHIEVOUS
IMPULSE
to pull the emergency brake.
NOW!

179

The <u>disappointment</u>
when the family fails to sing
hallelujahs at your return.

180

THE <u>YEARNING</u>
FOR HISTORIC
STATURE.

181

THE FEAR
OF A MAJOR
LIFE CHANGE.

182

The pride that
your present was the
best of them all.

183

THE DREAD OF
BEING SINGLED OUT
AT CUSTOMS.

184

The sense of
LOSTNESS
in the universe.

185

The astonishment at the
neighbor's unexpected
friendliness.

186

THE EXASPERATION AT YOUR OWN COWARDICE.

187

The ambition to finally make the high score on this level.

188

The panic that you might not make it to the bathroom on time.

189

THE JEALOUSY OF STRANGERS HOLDING HANDS.

190

The tickled feeling when young people think you're sort of cool for some inexplicable reason.

191

THE
FEAR OF LOSING
YOUR JOB.

192

The joy when
the guests admire you stirring
the risotto.

193

The exasperation
at botching the plain old
Sunday pound cake.

194

The

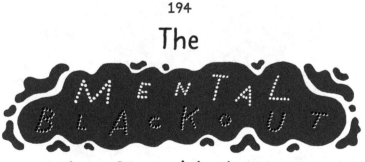

when forced to leave an
entry in a guestbook.

195

The <u>longing</u> to overcome
all your inhibitions
for once.

196

The <u>triumph</u> of overcoming
all your inhibitions
for once.

197

The
⋜⋅GRATIFICATION⋅⋟
of having spoiled your sons
rotten, thus raising the
bar impossibly high
for their wives.

198

The <u>confusion</u>
following a very
vivid dream.

THE

SUDDEN

WHILE GAZING

OUT A

TRAIN WINDOW.

200

The *affection*
at a child's
clumsiness.

201

The
envy of parents
with children.

202

THE EMOTION WHEN
ROYAL WEDDINGS ARE
SHOWN ON TELEVISION.

203

The hope that the jerk who
stole your bike will crash it
and die an agonizing death.

204

The annoyance at
guests who show up
much too early.

205

The satisfaction following physical exhaustion.

206

The disappointment when no one notices anything.

207

The hankering to pinch the girl in front of you.

208

THE ENJOYMENT OF A TEMPER TANTRUM.

209

THE PANIC THAT SOMEONE ELSE MIGHT HAVE GOTTEN THIS BRILLIANT IDEA LONG AGO AND SOON IT'LL MAKE HIM RICH.

210
THE HELLISH ORDEAL
OF YOUR CHILD'S FIRST
DAY OF SCHOOL.

211
The joy that your
granddaughter is your
spitting image.

212
Remorse over
something that happened
ages ago.

213
The pride at having taken this clock
apart, cleaned it, and put it back
together in perfect working order.

214
THE BITTERNESS
OF A LONELY
SUNDAY.

215

The _envy_ of
the cat's total
relaxation.

216

THE PRIDE AT BEING
TOTALLY ON THE MARK
FOR ONCE.

217

The
perplexity at
her silence.

218

The

ASTONISHMENT

at having sudden visions of the
Virgin Mary when you finally start
wearing your contact lenses again.

219

The <u>wicked</u> <u>glee</u> when
your best friend's husband
also has an affair.

220

THE

SENSE OF

WITH YOURSELF.

221

THE

TEMPTATION TO CROSS

A THRESHOLD.

222

The <u>delight</u> that
one out of a hundred photos
came out really well.

223

*THE BAFFLEMENT
AT THE SLAP IN THE FACE
YOU JUST GOT.*

224

**THE HESITATION
BEFORE SENDING AN
IMPORTANT E-MAIL.**

225

The happiness of
fulfilling one of your mother's
lifelong dreams.

226

The annoyance that, as
the older brother, you're always
responsible for everything.

227

The pride at helping the
stranger next to you in the plane
cope with her fear of flying.

228

The _remorse_
at having done someone
a terrible injustice.

229

The _fear_
that the worst is
yet to come.

230

The
gratitude that she
listened to you.

231

THE _AMAZEMENT_
AT HOW MUCH HOT AIR PEOPLE
MANAGE TO PRODUCE.

232

THE _COURAGE_
TO LEAVE THINGS
OPEN.

233

The _jealousy_ of the bimbos at the next table who get so much better service from the good-looking waiter.

234

The <u>tenderness</u> at the sight of your husband peeling tangerines for you.

235

The

of waking up one morning as someone called Leaf Warrior. Or Rain Dancer.

236

The <u>pride</u> of discovering you've got some talent after all.

237
The hope that the guy over there will finally stfu.

238
The childish pleasure of getting the first e-mail in your life at the age of seventy-three.

239
The shame of having wished your little sister dead when you were kids.

240
The astonishment at life's lucky coincidences.

241
The loneliness of being away from home.

242

THE EXASPERATION
AT MAKING THE SAME STUPID MISTAKE ALL OVER AGAIN.

243

The insatiable yearning for the latest iPad.

244

The consternation when you can't remember that damn name for the life of you.

245

THE GRIM SATISFACTION OF HAVING ENEMIES.

246

The PANICKY FEAR of arriving late.

247

The <u>awe</u> every
time you see the
Cologne Cathedral.

248

THE

AT GETTING UP EARLY
FOR ONCE.

249

The <u>resignation</u>
over the cat's failure to show
any kind of gratitude.

250

The <u>awkwardness</u> of
being a football hater invited
to watch football.

251

The _shame_
over the mediocrity
of your work.

252

The _hope_
that he'll text
you back.

253

THE _FEAR_ THAT
YOU'LL NEVER FALL
IN LOVE AGAIN.

254

The _wonderment_
at always being able
to love anew.

255

The _misgiving_ that
this remark might make you
seem anti-Semitic.

256

THE HOPE OF BEING FOUND.

257
The shyness
about asking for an
autograph.

258
THE GLOATING FEELING
WHEN CELEBRITIES' RELATIONSHIPS
DON'T WORK OUT.

259
The urge to brush
the dandruff off the shoulders
of the man up there.

260
The dignity
of trying on a uniform from
a costume rental.

261
The longing for
everything to turn out just
like it does in that song.

262
The _fear_ of
totally messing up your
performance.

263
The _contrition_
at failing yet again to
buy organic fruit.

264
The _pride_ in your all-around
education when you already know all
the answers on the quiz shows.

265
THE _GLEE_
AT CAUSING
CONFUSION.

266
The _anger_ at
yourself for not exercising
again today.

267

THE DISMAY
AT YOUR OWN
VANITY.

268

The emotion when
a friend is able to speak again
after a stroke.

269

The anticipation on the eve
of your eighth birthday...
and all the rest.

270

The horror
at your fantasies
of murder.

271

The gladness
at unexpected
friendship.

272

THE <u>ANNOYANCE</u> AT HAVING FAILED TO ASSERT YOURSELF JUST NOW.

273

The

EMBARRASSMENT

of sending an e-mail to the wrong person.

274

The <u>delight</u> at the way your parents are just sitting there holding hands.

275

THE <u>PANIC</u> RIGHT BEFORE THE THE DEADLINE.

276

The <u>doubt</u> whether
everything actually was the
way you remember it.

277

The <u>unease</u> at the thought that
even this memory might be
something you made up yourself.

278

THE <u>PRIDE</u> AT HAVING
PULLED YET ANOTHER
ALL-NIGHTER.

279

THE <u>SHAME</u> AT
YOUR LACK OF INTEREST
IN POLITICS.

280

The <u>bafflement</u> when your
German colleague tries to explain
to you what schadenfreude is.

281

THE HOPE
OF
WORLD FAME.

282

The sentimentality when you're cleaning
out the basement and find old love letters
from guys you'd almost forgotten.

283

The worry that
you haven't said hi to all
your guests.

284

The relief
following a difficult
conversation.

285

The aversion to
getting out of bed in this
rotten weather.

286

THE <u>INCREDULOUSNESS</u> THAT THEY STILL DON'T GET IT.

287

The <u>happiness</u> of noticing that your ear is all warm after the phone conversation and he's still with you a little bit.

288

THE <u>SADNESS</u> AT HAVING TO DEPART SOON.

289

The <u>hatred</u> of wet dogs on the train.

290

The <u>wanderlust</u> that follows rain.

THE ENVY OF JERKS.

292

THE *TESTINESS* OF HAVING TO WORRY ABOUT EVERY SINGLE LITTLE DETAIL BECAUSE OTHERWISE NOTHING WOULD GET DONE.

293

The WORRY, despite everything the doctor says, that you're suffering from a sinister disease no one has ever had before.

294

The annoyance over this squandered afternoon.

295

The p<u>ani</u>c
when your partner stops
breathing in his sleep.

296

The j<u>o</u>y when
the UPS guy
rings.

297

The <u>irritation</u> at
certain quirks of someone
you love.

298

The <u>affection</u>
for those same quirks a
moment later.

299

THE <u>FEAR</u> OF ADMITTING
TO YOURSELF THAT YOU DON'T
LOVE YOUR CHILDREN.

300

THE DISTRESS AT YOUR FIRST GRAY HAIRS.

301

The envy
of wrinkles on an
old person's face.

302

The queasiness before
the meeting that will
decide everything.

303

The sadness
of realizing how
finite life is.

304

The delight over a
perfect specimen found
mushroom hunting.

305

THE
HORROR OF HAGGLING
IN BAZAARS.

306

*The satisfaction
of having talked everyone
into submission.*

307

THE SADNESS
AT THE SIGHT OF
GREAT BEAUTY.

308

THE WORRY
WHETHER THE CONDOM
WILL HOLD.

309

*The anticipation
of a
baby's smile.*

310

THE

LONGING

TO SEEM ENIGMATIC AND FULL OF MYSTERY.

311

THE <u>DISMAY</u> AT DIALING THE WRONG NUMBER THREE TIMES IN A ROW.

312

THE <u>FURY</u>
AT A
MISHAP.

313

The <u>pride</u> of getting the show on the road again.

314

The superiority of
appearing for a meeting in
a perfectly fitting suit.

315

**THE RAGE AT
LOUD SUPER BOWL
PARTIES.**

316

THE

Yearning

FOR THE WORLD TO
STOP TURNING AND THIS PERFECT SUMMER
AFTERNOON TO LAST FOREVER.

317

The
shame of unearned
success.

318

THE BLISS OF
SLIPPING INTO A FRESHLY
MADE BED.

319

The anger at
yourself for sneaking another
smoke after all.

320

The grim
satisfaction of ultimately
being the better person.

321

The
thankfulness for
having friends.

322

The relief
brought on by an attack
of self-pity.

323
The pride at finding the perfect place for your new hammock.

324
THE MISTRUST TOWARD PEOPLE WHO ARE ALWAYS SAYING THANK YOU.

325
The bemusement at young urban women carrying around big water bottles in massive backpacks.

326
The fear of old-age oblivion.

327
The shock at how much you've aged.

328

The
itch to cut
in line.

329

The **worry** that you just
completely humiliated yourself
with that remark.

330

THE **LONGING**

FOR WHAT

HAS PASSED.

331

The

SMUGNESS

of recognizing German tourists
by the way they stake out the best
pool chairs in the morning.

332
THE ETERNAL
DISSATISFACTION WITH
THE MANUSCRIPT.

333
The satisfaction
of running faster than
all the rest.

334
The elation at a taste that
suddenly transports you back
to a morning in your childhood.

335
THE EAGER ANTICIPATION
WAITING FOR THE PHOTOS
FROM THE PHOTO BOOTH.

336
The unease
at having made up
prematurely.

337

The happiness when the contract comes back signed.

338

THE STRANGE, IRRATIONAL URGE TO RIDE THE ROLLER COASTER AGAIN EVEN THOUGH YOU'RE ALREADY FEELING SICK.

339

The

that people thought that was funny just now.

340

The envy that the woman in the passenger seat has such a good sense of direction.

THE SHAME

AT SEEING THE GLASS HALF-EMPTY RATHER THAN HALF-FULL, BUT NOT SAYING IT, BECAUSE THEN THEY'D JUST TAKE YOU AS AN INCORRIGIBLE PESSIMIST WHO'S USUALLY RIGHT BUT JUST MAKES THINGS HARD FOR HIMSELF, AND WHO WANTS THAT?

342
The gratitude for inspiration.

343
The <u>hope</u> for even more clicks on your new website.

344
<u>Satisfaction</u> over winning the battle for the middle armrest in the airplane.

345
The <u>abashment</u> around successful friends.

346
THE <u>HOPE</u> THAT SHE'LL COME BACK.

347

The _shock_ of realizing that
you're not the good guy
this time.

348

The _pride_ of
being complimented
on your hands.

349

The _anger_
at bad-smelling men
on the train.

350

The _longing_ for him to
suddenly get up, come over, and
sit down next to you.

351

The _shock_ of
not liking yourself
anymore.

352

The p<u>ride</u> of ordering in
Spanish at a Mexican restaurant for
the first time at the age of eleven.

353

The <u>happiness</u>
of being
back home.

354

THE <u>IMPATIENCE</u> OF WONDERING
WHEN THE HELL SHE'LL BE DONE IN
THE BATHROOM.

355

The profound
<u>abhorrence</u> of the theory
of evolution.

356

The <u>diffidence</u> when, yet again, your
intellectual friends go off on some
topic you can't contribute to.

357

THE LONGING
TO
READ MINDS.

358

THE RELIEF
THAT YOU CAN'T
READ MINDS.

359

The disappointment
that that smile was meant
for someone else.

360

The joy of finding
old friends again after
a long time.

361

THE FEAR
OF YOUR LIFE
IMPLODING.

362

The exasperation at people
who are constantly complaining
about the weather.

363

The <u>relief</u> on your first date
when she orders the osso buco
and not just a "nice salad,"

364

The <u>terror</u>
of the never-ending
vicious circle.

365

THE <u>RELIEF</u> WHEN
SHE CHANGES THE SUBJECT
BEFORE REALIZING THAT
EVERYTHING YOU WERE
SAYING ABOUT IT WAS
TOTAL BULLSHIT.

366

THE <u>FURY</u> WHEN HE JUST PLAIN STOOD YOU UP THAT EVENING.

367

The <u>astonishment</u> at all the hair that man up there has on his arms.

368

The <u>pleasant</u> <u>anticipation</u> of a perfectly normal, quiet Tuesday.

369

The *GUILTY FEELING* of thinking all Mexicans are illegals, all blacks are drug dealers, and all Middle Eastern-looking people are suspicious.

370

The _resentment_ that none of your friends came, even though it would have meant a lot to you.

371

The _warm fuzzy feeling_ about strangers' old family photos.

372

THE PRIDE IN YOUR CHILDREN'S INTELLIGENCE.

373

The thrill of anticipation before spilling a secret.

374

The _relief_ of not meeting anyone from your old gang.

375

The shock of
realizing how fundamentally
simple everything is.

376

THE TREPIDATION OF

HAVING TO GO OUT IN A MOMENT

AND TELL THE FAMILY

THAT YOUR PATIENT

DIED

ON THE OPERATING TABLE.

377

The envy
of your big sister's
perfection.

378

The fear
of drunken kids on the
train platform.

379

The _teariness_ over
a child's wise insights into
the way of the world.

380

THE <u>COWARDICE</u> THAT

KEEPS YOU FROM ADMITTING THAT

YOU DON'T LOVE YOUR SPOUSE.

381

The <u>annoyance</u> at obtrusive
compliments from men your age
about your fine head of hair.

382

The <u>worry</u>
that ultimately you're
much too indulgent.

383

THE <u>JOY</u>
OF LAUGHING WITH
YOUR PARENTS.

384

*The hope
that nobody noticed
that fart.*

385

*The hopefulness at
the sight of elderly couples
holding hands.*

386

The anger at having
to constantly justify
everything you do.

387

*The shame of not
liking all your nieces and
nephews the same.*

388

THE BRIEF PANIC WHEN YOU
MAKE A FACE AND WORRY IT'LL
FREEZE THAT WAY.

ENVY

of other people's hickeys.

391

THE <u>EMBARRASSMENT</u>
OF USING THE WORD *MIDGET*
IN FRONT OF A DWARF,

392

*The <u>pride</u> at
having shown some
courage for once.*

393

The impotent

RAGE

*at the subcompact crawling along
up there in front of you, constantly
signaling but never turning.*

394

THE SUPERIOR FEELING ABOUT BACHELOR PARTIES.

395

THE HOPE OF SAYING SOMETHING INTELLIGENT ONE DAY.

396

The resentment of colleagues' undeserved success.

397

That angry why-me feeling at a life filled with minefields.

398

The happiness of finding the favorite scarf you lost.

399

The <u>ANNOYANCE</u> THAT THE WAITER THINKS YOUR UNINTENTIONALLY LARGE TIP IS JUST YOU SHOWING OFF.

400

The <u>good</u> <u>mood</u> that follows pleasant daydreams.

401

The <u>disappointment</u> at your children's boundless egotism.

402

The ssself-contempt while checking every other minute to see if anyone's finally reacted to your incredibly original Facebook post. 👎

403

THE <u>AMAZEMENT</u> AT
HOW MUCH SHE CAN DRINK.
WITHOUT FALLING DOWN.

404

The
ANGER
at your old teacher who told you
in 1978 that none of you would live
past thirty-five, what with
nuclear war and all that.

405

The <u>appreciation</u> of
sympathy when you're
feeling really lousy.

406

The <u>happiness</u> of waking up
and hearing him clatter dishes in
the kitchen, making breakfast.

407

The hope
that the cops won't
make Joe talk.

408

THE PANIC OF SEARCHING
FOR A GOOD PLACE TO
HIDE THE LOOT.

409

The dread of the boss
asking how much
you got done today.

410

THE HOPE OF
GROWING A FEW MORE
INCHES AFTER ALL.

411

The bitterness
over the treason of your
most loyal acolyte.

412

THE DREAD
OF NODDING
OFF.

413

THE FEAR
THAT NIGHT COULD
LAST FOREVER.

414

THE DISMAY WHEN
YOU REALIZE YOU'VE ACQUIRED
SOME ANNOYING TICS.

415

The

of being her
sugar daddy.

416

The rage at
your parents' bland
condescension.

417

THE GRIM SATISFACTION
OF REMOVING BIRD DROPPINGS
FROM THE PAINT JOB.

418

The fear
of being reborn as a frog
in your next life.

419

THE WORRY
THAT YOUR SUIT LOOKS
LIKE A COSTUME.

420

THE EUPHORIA
THAT A TASK HAS YOU FULLY IN
YOUR ELEMENT.

421

THE HAPPINESS
OF BEING FOUND AGAIN IN THE CROWD
AT THE OPEN-AIR CONCERT.

422

The _anger_ at
people who don't clean up
after their dogs.

423

THE HOPE
THAT HE'LL DIE
SOON.

424

THE FRIGHT
DURING THE
SIREN TEST.

425

The satisfaction
of breaking
a heart.

426

The

of rummaging through a strange
refrigerator and drawing conclusions
about these people's lifestyles.

427

THE <u>UNEASINESS</u>

BEFORE YOUR FIRST

VACATION TOGETHER.

428

THE <u>FEAR</u>

OF BEING WRONGLY

CONVICTED.

429

The <u>panic</u>
that it could all
come out.

430

The <u>bliss</u> that you
can whine to your wife about
the world's depravity.

431

The <u>mistrust</u> of
wondering why that guy
just smiled at you.

432

The <u>suspense</u> as to
whether she'll come up to your
apartment later on.

433

The <u>hatred</u> of that
pimple on your forehead,
today of all days!

434

The <u>relief</u> when
things don't turn out
quite so badly after all.

435

THE <u>WORRY</u>
THAT YOU YIELDED
TOO SOON.

436

The
<u>consternation</u> that it
had to rain today.

437

The <u>bitterness</u>
following the loss in
the semifinals.

438

THE <u>EAGERNESS</u>
FOR THE FIRST COFFEE
IN THE MORNING.

439

The <u>shudder</u> at the
thought of what the neighbors
are doing up there.

440

THE DELIGHT IN SILLY THINGS YOU DO TOGETHER THAT NO ONE ELSE UNDERSTANDS, MUCH LESS THINKS ARE FUNNY.

441
THE INCOMPREHENSION OF PEOPLE WITHOUT THE SLIGHTEST SENSE OF HUMOR.

442
The _relief_ of having
a smoke in your car first
thing after the party.

443
The _trepidation_ before the
tango taster course you stupidly
let yourself get talked into.

444

while
eating French fries.

445

THE <u>LONGING</u>
TO BE A MOB BOSS WITH
A HEART OF GOLD.

446

The <u>pride</u> when you picture the incredible talents your newborn is bound to have.

447

The <u>discomfiture</u> of stripping down to your bathing suit at the beach.

448

The <u>ire</u> at the smiley at the end of the sentence. ☹

449

THE <u>OUTRAGE</u> AT GETTING TURNED AWAY BY THE BOUNCER DESPITE YOUR ÜBERCOOL OUTFIT.

450

THE PRIDE
AT A LIE
WELL LIED.

451

**THE
LONGING FOR
A HICKEY.**

452

The indignation
at finding typos in books
and magazines.

453

The shyness that keeps you
from turning back and asking her
for her cell phone number.

454

The thrill
at your daughter's
clever question.

455

The

at your own
stupidity.

456

THE GUILTY FEELING
OF OFFENDING SOMEONE WITH
A THOUGHTLESS REMARK.

457

The astonishment that
people still say hi to you
despite everything.

458

The consternation of suddenly
realizing you're much more like
your parents than you'd hoped.

459

The _envy_ of
the flirting smokers
outside the pub.

460

_The resentment at the
smokers for leaving you all by
yourself at the table._

461

THE HAPPINESS OF
HANGING OUT WITH
YOUR BEST BUDDIES.

462

The _mystification_
that there are certain people
you just don't like.

463

_The joy
in your
work._

464

THE FEAR
OF GETTING
STARTED.

465

THE DESPERATION OF
HAVING TO DECIDE RIGHT NOW,
THIS VERY SECOND.

466

The curiosity to see what
will happen if I press that
red button there.

467

The barely controllable
urge to smack that kid
upside the head.

468

The fury that someone
had to cough right in the middle
of the pianissimo.

469

The lifelong <u>yearning</u>
to be taken seriously
by your father.

470

The <u>dismay</u> at
having forgotten something
very important.

471

THE <u>PRIDE</u> IN YOUR OWN BEARD.

472

The inexplicable
<u>aversion</u> to answering this
one stupid e-mail.

473

The <u>diffidence</u>
at having to make a complaint
in a foreign language.

474

THE <u>BITTERNESS</u> AT
ALWAYS GETTING A
RAW DEAL IN LIFE.

475

The <u>hope</u>
that this fear
is unfounded.

476

The sudden

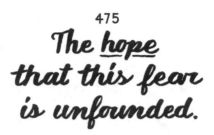

when you finally make yourself
clean out the basement and throw out
your old exercise books.

477

The <u>annoyance</u> at
being the first to blink
in the staring game.

478

THE
<u>ANTICIPATION</u> OF
A PRESENT.

479

The <u>dismay</u> when your kid has a temper tantrum out of the blue.

480

The <u>warm</u> <u>fuzzy</u> <u>feeling</u> about yourself when you take the spider outside instead of squishing it.

481

The

of being hungover the next day.

482

THE _DESPAIR_
WHEN ALL THE SHOPS ARE
ALREADY CLOSED.

483

THE

WHEN FACED WITH
THE EMPTY PAGE.

484

The _love_ of your brother
when you recognize
yourself in him.

485

The _happiness_
of lounging on the
sofa together.

486

THE

WHEN YOU
LEARN OF HIS
DEATH.

487

The anticipation of the new mail-order catalog.

488

The remorse that you'd given your child the blame.

489

THE HOPE

NOT TO BE ALONE IN
YOUR OLD AGE.

490

The <u>Protestant</u> <u>misgiving</u>
that this lucky streak (undeserved,
of course) will soon end.

491

*THE <u>PANIC</u> OF FEELING
A LUMP IN YOUR ARMPIT
ONE MORNING.*

492

THE <u>TREPIDATION</u> WHEN
THE DOCTOR SAYS: "WE'LL HAVE
THAT FIXED IN NO TIME."

493

The

of being thick as thieves
for the moment.

494

The <u>incomprehension</u>
when a violent crime happens
at your own doorstep.

495

THE <u>PLEASURE</u> WHEN HE GIVES
YOU EARRINGS FOR ONCE
INSTEAD OF ANOTHER "NICE TRIP."

496

The personal
<u>disappointment</u> that it's
November again already.

497

The

when
know-it-alls
screw up.

THE
UNQUENCHABLE

YEARNING

FOR APPLAUSE
AND HYMNS
OF PRAISE.

499

The _envy_
of other people's
talent.

500

The
passion for
speed.

501

THE GRIM _GRATIFICATION_
OF SQUEEZING
PIMPLES.

502

THE _GRIEF_
OVER THE BREAKUP OF YOUR
FAVORITE BAND.

503

The _pride_
at having said no
for once.

504

The _envy_
of your siblings'
affluence.

505

The _relief_ at not
growing up in a slum
in Mumbai.

506

The
resentment of fuzz on
your favorite coat.

507

The _joyful_
anticipation of your
vacation together.

508

The not entirely
unfounded _fear_ of being
a dreadful bore.

509
The vague certainty
of being a key figure in a
global conspiracy.

510
The fear of divulging
secrets in your sleep, or
even naming names.

511
THE ITCH TO PRESS
ALL THE DOOR BUZZERS
AT ONCE.

512
The
impotent rage
at the umpire.

513
The contrition of knowing you'd wish
for all kinds of things from the good
fairy, just not world peace.

514

The joy of getting praised to the skies by your friends.

515

The diffidence
about taking photos of natives
when traveling abroad.

516

The jealousy of friends
who seem to succeed effortlessly
at everything in life.

517

The profound
❧ RELIEF ❧
at discovering there's pasta
and risotto in other countries too.
Not as good as Mama's,
of course, but still.

518

*The impatience
to go to work
today.*

519

THE RAGE

WHEN DEALING WITH A
SMART-ALECKY KID.

520

The tenderness at
the sight of a bed filled
with crumbs.

521

*The shock when an
old friend makes a sudden
declaration of love.*

522

THE CONTENTMENT

AFTER THE CRY
OF RAGE.

523

The pride at having already achieved things in life after all.

524

The doubt whether that has any value at all.

525

The attack of homesickness while still planning your vacation.

526

THE SENSE OF TRIUMPH AT NOT WIMPING OUT ON THE MOUNTAIN BIKE.

527

THE FURY AT HAVING BEEN UNDERESTIMATED YET AGAIN.

528
The gratitude
over a
small favor.

529
The <u>despair</u> at
having to let go before
it even started.

530
The <u>shock</u> that not
everyone in foreign countries
speaks English.

531
THE <u>EMBARRASSMENT</u> ABOUT THE
TOKEN APPLE IN THE MIDST OF ALL THE
JUNK FOOD IN YOUR SHOPPING CART.

532
THE <u>SELF-PITY</u> OF
LYING ALL ALONE AT HOME
IN BED WITH THE FLU.

533

The <u>annoyance</u>
that today of all days there's
nothing but crap on TV.

534

The <u>ire</u> at the
manufacturers of fiddly
plastic packaging.

535

The <u>annoyance</u>
at your teenage kids'
bad posture.

536

THE <u>FEAR</u>

THAT THE PIPE

WILL BURST.

537

The <u>embarrassment</u>
of wearing too short a skirt
in windy weather.

538

THE DESPAIR THAT YOU'LL NEVER, EVER BE AS THIN AS THOSE MODELS.

539

The disappointment when your husband doesn't even notice the little scratches you got working in the garden.

540

THE SORROW AT THE SIGHT OF A DYING LIONESS IN THE SERENGETI.

541

The dread of suffering from anatadaephobia (the constant fear that somewhere, somehow, a duck is watching you).

542

The
envy of the tenth-
grade guys.

543

The

FRUSTRATION

of how exhausting it is
to act halfway cool
all the time.

544

THE HOPE THAT
THEY'LL ALWAYS BE THERE
FOR YOU.

545

The terror
of being buried
alive.

546

The <u>thankfulness</u> that someone's holding tight to the dog's leash.

547

The <u>outrage</u> at people who cut in line.

548

The <u>regret</u> over something that got broken.

549

THE

RELIEF

THAT HE DIDN'T FLIP OUT, THOUGH GOODNESS KNOWS HE'D HAVE HAD EVERY REASON TO.

THE ANGER AT GETTING KICKED OUT OF THE BAR TOO EARLY.

551

The
❧ BLISS ❧
of finally getting a
peaceful moment to yourself
in the bathroom.

552

The <u>fury</u> when
the other kids won't let
you play with them.

553

The anxiety
that keeps you from
admitting a lie.

554

The <u>hope</u> that
this one time you won't
disappoint her.

555

The <u>satisfaction</u>
in your own
perspicacity.

556

The
EMBARRASSMENT
of staring right at the breasts
of that woman up there,
and of course
she noticed it.

557

THE <u>SPEECHLESSNESS</u> WHEN HE STOLE YOUR PUNCHLINE.

558

THE BITTER <u>GRATIFICATION</u> THAT
EVERYTHING TURNED OUT JUST AS
BADLY AS YOU'D ALWAYS FEARED.

559

The <u>misanthropy</u> sparked
by all the people
in the shopping center.

560

THE <u>ENJOYMENT</u>

OF BRIEFLY WITHDRAWING

YOUR AFFECTIONS.

561

The <u>exhilaration</u> of
smelling the beach grass the first
time you walk on the dunes.

562

The <u>wrath</u>
at the bearer of
bad news.

563

The youngest brother's
<u>indignation</u> that he was always
the underdog back then.

564

THE INDIGNATION THAT YOUR
LITTLE BROTHER GOT EVERYTHING HANDED
TO HIM ON A SILVER PLATTER.

565

The mystification at
the strange problems
grown-ups have.

566

The enjoyment
of the first really hot
summer day.

567

The fear that
your parents will have
another fight.

568

The relief
that the secret's
finally out.

569

The
PANIC
of realizing that the darling little
Italian B&B where you'll be vacationing
for three weeks doesn't have
an Internet connection.

570

The <u>happiness</u> of
hosing down the veranda
in March.

571

The <u>surprise</u>
when you don't feel
the pain.

572

The <u>surprise</u>
when you feel it a
moment later.

573

The discomfort when
your boss's name appears
on the phone display.

574

The bewilderment
at the marriage proposal
out of the blue.

575

The worry that
you've said "I love you"
too often.

576

THE

RARING-TO-GO FEELING
AFTER TAKING
A SHOWER.

577
THE DREAD OF
HAVING TO TAKE A LIFE IN
SELF-DEFENSE SOMEDAY.

578
The
annoyance at unfunny
Facebook comments.

579
THE ENVY
OF YOUR BEST FRIEND'S
NATURAL GLAMOUR.

580
The disappointment that no
matter how hard you try, you'll
never be as glamorous as she is.

581
Impotent despair
faced with the pile of
unpaid bills.

582

THE

THAT THERE MIGHT BE
SOMETHING TO THE NOTION
OF REINCARNATION.

583

*The satisfaction
when looking
in the mirror.*

584

The
fear of
dying.

585

THE JOY OF
BEING SMILED AT BY
A STRANGER.

586

THE ANGER AT THE WAY
EVERYONE REFUSED TO ADMIT THE PROJECT
WAS DOOMED AND JUST KEPT AT IT.

587

The powerless feeling
when, once again, no one takes
the blame for the disaster.

588

The apprehension
of losing everything in
one fell swoop.

589

The longing
to share your pain
with him.

590

The worry that this
question will wake
sleeping dogs.

591

𝕿he _envy_
of the people
out there in
the sunshine.

592

THE <u>GLEE</u> THAT YOU DON'T HAVE TO LEAVE THE HOUSE TODAY AND FREEZE YOUR BUTT OFF OUT THERE.

593

The

at how long it takes
to get there.

594

The

at how little time it takes
to get back.

595

The p<u>ain</u> of
being an unplanned
child.

596

The <u>shock</u> of realizing
the wrong person is
in love with you.

597

The <u>mystification</u>
as to whom the kid got
that from.

598

The <u>anger</u> that
it had to start pouring
right now.

599

THE <u>JOY</u>

OF TRAVELING WITH

NO BAGGAGE.

600

The devastation
over your own
mediocrity.

601

The anticipation of
getting somewhere with
her this evening.

602

The insatiable
greed for electronic
love notes.

603

The satisfaction
with the year's
first sunburn.

604

The
embarrassment about
this sunburn.

605

The <u>confidence</u> that there's a grand scheme of things after all.

606

The <u>abhorrence</u> of people with disabilities.

607

The <u>shame</u> you feel about it.

608

The <u>rage</u> at your little sister's lame arguments for who gets what room in the new house.

609

The <u>impatience</u> for the Easter egg hunt.

610

The
amazement
at being loved
so dearly
despite your
mediocrity.

611

The _sentimentality_
of recognizing your parents
in your own quirks.

612

THE _WORRY_ THAT
THERE MIGHT NOT BE ENOUGH
FOR EVERYONE.

613

The mounting _irritation_ at
the child dawdling so provokingly
as he puts on his shoes.

614

The pride
in being a
nerd.

615

The disappointment
of not being among
the initiated.

616

THE SHAME AT
HAVING ACTED COOLER
THAN YOU ARE.

617

The

at those jokes of your husband's
that never change but make
you laugh every time.

618
THE CONSTANT <u>WORRY</u> THAT SOMETHING MIGHT HAPPEN TO YOUR CHILDREN.

619
The <u>envy</u> of the youthful appearance of your former classmates.

620
The <u>loneliness</u> of the first night in the new apartment.

621
The <u>bitterness</u> that she broke her promise after all.

622
The <u>pleasure</u> when your favorite song comes on the radio.

623

THE FEAR THAT THE MEDICATIONS WON'T WORK.

624

THE COMFORT OF SNIFFING AT GRANDMA'S OLD FUR COLLAR.

625

The annoyance at not getting a word in edgewise in the discussion.

626

The unshakeable JOIE DE VIVRE in difficult times.

627

THE DREAD
OF YOUR OWN
HOTHEADEDNESS.

628

The
Sentimentality
when you can hardly tear
yourself away from watching
your sleeping children.

629

The jealousy of the
colleague who's fifteen years
younger than you.

630

THE ETERNAL
UNEASE AT THE CASH
MACHINE.

631
THE HAPPINESS
OF HAVING FOUND YOUR
PLACE IN LIFE.

632
The envy of
people who have something
resembling enemies.

633
The bloodlust toward the cat
that just sampled all the freshly
fried Swedish meatballs.

634
The pride you feel
for your husband, just seeing
him standing up there.

635
THE
DOUBTS IN YOUR
OWN FIDELITY.

636

*The satisfaction
of having been
helpful.*

637

The dismay
that it was all just
a mistake.

638

THE RELIEF OF
GETTING NEWS YOU'D
HOPED FOR.

639

The

of the bunch of friends having a
nice time at the next table.

640

*The irritation
of standing
in line.*

641

The relief
that no one
asked.

642

The despair
of getting completely
stalled on a project.

643

The

FURY

over the "little hike" your husband
dreamed up that turned out to be a fixed
rope route above terrifying abysses.

644

*The <u>relief</u>
at an unexpected
reprieve.*

645

The slight

about the seventy-seven virgins
waiting in that other paradise.

646

THE <u>FEAR</u> OF BEING THE
ONLY ONE WITH A GRASP OF THE
FULL REPERCUSSIONS.

647

THE <u>PANIC</u> AT HAVING
TO GO HOME AND CONFESS
EVERYTHING.

THE POWER LESS NESS AGAINST DARK THOUGHTS WHEN YOU CAN'T SLEEP NIGHTS.

649

The <u>disappointment</u>
that your present was
totally off-base.

650

*THE <u>ENVY</u> OF YOUR
COWORKER WHOSE GIRLFRIEND
IS CONSTANTLY CALLING.*

651

The

 *malicious pleasure*

*when your coworker's girlfriend
calls to ask why he isn't
heading home yet.*

652

The <u>sadness</u> that
no one is calling you to ask when
you'll finally be coming home.

653

The
discomfort of
telling a lie.

654

The satisfaction
after wrapping up
your work.

655

The helplessness
of not knowing what they're
talking about over there.

656

The horror at how carelessly
your neighbor with kids
stores his shotgun.

657

The relief that
you did decide to light a votive
just now in the cathedral.

658

The <u>shame</u> of praising
other people just to feel
better about yourself.

659

THE <u>PRIDE</u> AT
ASKING THE RIGHT
QUESTIONS.

660

The <u>rage</u> at
getting woken up by a completely
pointless phone call.

661

The <u>relief</u>
when the ambulance
finally comes.

662

The <u>frisson</u> of
reading the safety information
on the airplane.

663

**THE DISMAY AT
HOW MUCH HYPOCRISY
THERE IS.**

664

The pride
in your children's
trust.

665

THE RAPTURE
OF CHANTING IN
THE STADIUM.

666

*THE DESPERATION WHEN EVERYONE
TELLS YOU YOU'VE GOT TO "FINALLY LET GO"
—AND YOU CAN'T.*

667

THE AMAZEMENT
AT HOW EASY IT WAS TO
LET GO AFTER ALL.

668

THE CHILDISH DEFIANCE WHEN
YOU MEET WITH A
BARRAGE OF CRITICISM.

669

The
shame at not having
answered her.

670

The
gratitude for her
understanding.

671

The
kick of
shoplifting.

672

The worry that
everything's already
been said.

673

The _anger_ at
the person who turned
out to be right.

674

The _hope_ of a brief,
cleansing fight rather than a long,
excruciating conflict.

675

The <u>uneasiness</u> of
realizing that a fight is
about to break out.

676

THE <u>URGE</u>

TO SWERVE INTO THE

GUARDRAIL.

677

The _longing_
for everything to be
nice and simple.

678

THE _FEAR_
OF SAYING THE
WRONG THING.

679

The eternal resentment of your parents, who are to blame for everything.

680

The despair
at not being able to
change anything.

681

THE
SELF-LOATHING
OF FRITTERING AWAY ANOTHER
ENTIRE DAY, EVEN THOUGH
THE DEADLINE IS BREATHING
DOWN YOUR NECK.

682

The
buoyant good mood upon
leaving the party.

683

The sadness
of being unable
to help.

684

THE PRIDE
IN YOUR
FATHER.

685

The disappointment
in the unreliability of your
grown-up children.

686

THE EXASPERATION AT FORGETTING
THE CLOTHES IN THE WASHING
MACHINE OVERNIGHT AGAIN.

687

The _enjoyment_ of the
candy bars you brought from home
when traveling abroad.

688

The _horror_ at
your own indifference to
war coverage on TV.

689

The sudden
pang at the smell of
frankincense.

690

THE _IMPATIENCE_
TO GET AN UNPLEASANT THING
OVER WITH ALREADY.

691

The _rage_ that up until the debt crisis
everyone played along cheerfully and counted
on getting away with it somehow.

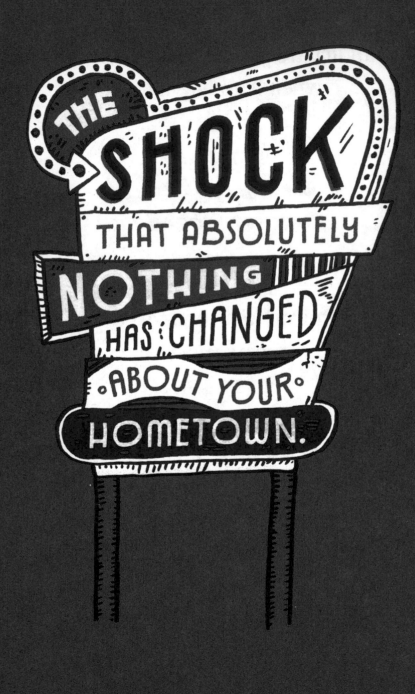

THE SHOCK THAT ABSOLUTELY NOTHING HAS CHANGED ABOUT YOUR HOMETOWN.

693

The <u>hope</u>
at the sight of
teenagers reading.

694

THE <u>CONTEMPT</u>
OF TEACHERS WITH
NO AUTHORITY.

695

The <u>annoyance</u>
when there's no answer
to your e-mail.

696

The <u>hope</u> that
a rash promise won't be
taken literally.

697

The <u>love</u> of
the old dog you got
at the age of ten.

698

The shock at your
own coldheartedness
just now.

699

The sobering
realization that this loss
is permanent.

700

The relief
of not having to
wear a tie.

701

THE
REGRET
THAT IT'S TOO LATE TO APOLOGIZE
TO YOUR DECEASED PARENTS FOR YOUR
ADOLESCENT BEHAVIOR.

702

THE INDIGNATION AT A THOUGHTLESS ACT BY YOUR PARTNER.

703

The

over little love notes on the breakfast table.

704

The
remorse at not having smiled back.

705

The distress of being unable to ease her suffering.

706

The
INCOMPREHENSION
as to how he could possibly think of giving me such a ridiculous present. He ought to know me better than that.

707

The **bitterness** at how the loudmouths and blowhards always get ahead faster than you.

708

The

when you watch the hero torturing someone on TV and feel nothing but a profound gratification.

709

The head-shaking amusement
while eavesdropping on teenagers
talking about zombie games.

710

*The pride at
having surmounted
a life crisis.*

711

The shyness that
keeps you from ringing
the doorbell.

712

The
WORRY
of not having a plausible
excuse to get out of a men's
group weekend involving
an Indian sweat lodge.

713

The fury at
your daughter's friend's
screwed-up parents.

714

**The
longing for more
inner serenity.**

715

The disappointment when your
truly generous tip fails to win
the charming waitress's heart.

716

The surprise
at actually
liking yourself.

717

The desperation of trying to
find an elegant excuse to finally skip
out on this insanely boring party.

718

THE _PITYING_ _DISGUST_ AT THE PASSED-OUT, VOMIT-COVERED BUM ON THE STREET.

719

The _trepidation_ at the sight of tall stacks of foreign-language books you have yet to work through.

720

The grim _certainty_ that you got infected long ago, even if your girlfriend thinks it's just your imagination.

721

The _bitterness_ at a lack of comments on Facebook.

722

THE SUDDEN _CALM_ AFTER A PAINFUL PARTING.

723

THE RELIEF AFTER THE EXAM.

724

THE NERVOUSNESS BEFORE THE FIRST DATE.

725

The contentment of a perfect afternoon.

726

The

when she classes you at a single glance as non-dangerous and non-interesting.

727

The happ<u>iness</u> that
everything is fine right now
the way it is.

728

THE <u>SHAME</u> AT HAVING

MADE FUN OF OTHER PEOPLE'S

DISABILITIES.

729

The

to go straight to the next
casino tonight and put all your
savings on twenty-eight.

730

The <u>incomprehension</u>
as to how anyone can
be that sloppy.

731

The envy
of other people's
secrets.

732

THE AWE

BEFORE THE ORIGINAL OF A

FAMOUS PAINTING.

733

The grief
when parents
die.

734

The desperation of
having to hit your parents
up for money again.

735

THE LONGING

FOR THE GOOD

OLD DAYS.

736

The _relief_
of hearing her voice
on the phone.

737

The _blazing_ _wrath_
when the hotline
puts you on hold.

738

The _fear_ that
you're taking a much too
casual approach.

739

The
__determination__ before
the first kiss.

740

The _fear_
of getting caught in
a speed trap.

741

The <u>happiness</u>
of burying your nose in
the cat's tummy fur.

742

The <u>fear</u> of having a twin brother
somewhere who's being sought as
a serial killer by the Interpol.

743

The <u>astonishment</u> when
someone you love suddenly
becomes a stranger to you.

744

THE <u>SATISFACTION</u>
OF HAVING GIVEN IT
YOUR ALL.

745

THE <u>DESPAIR</u> AT
ALWAYS BEING THE SLOWEST
IN THE CLASS.

747

*The panic at
the inability to hold on to
this one moment.*

748

THE PERPLEXITY OVER
AN UNEXPECTED DECLARATION
OF LOVE.

749

The

AMAZEMENT

*at how simple
everything is
all of a sudden.*

750

The annoyance with
yourself when you've given
much too big a tip again.

751

The <u>self-satisfaction</u> at not lighting yourself a cigarette after all.

752

The <u>disappointment</u> when all your good advice is thrown to the winds.

753

THE <u>TRIUMPH</u> OF YIELDING TO YOUR OWN MEGALOMANIA.

754

The <u>bewilderment</u> at how someone with no clue can be so confident.

755

The <u>envy</u> of all the people who can actually call it a day when they leave the office.

756

The longing to just get
out at the next stop and
start all over again.

757

THE SUPPRESSED
AGGRESSION WHEN STANDING
ON THE ESCALATOR.

758

The fear of
losing someone
you love.

759

The relief of
not being alone in
your sorrow.

760

The bliss when you can
crawl into your parents' bed
and go on sleeping there.

761

The desperate sense
of being to blame for your
parents' separation.

762

THE

IRRITATION AT AFFLUENT KIDS'

CONSTANT WHINING.

763

The outrage
that your life partner has
predeceased you.

764

The pleasure at
a compliment you've
never heard before.

765

The joy of waking up
and realizing you get to doze
for another half an hour.

766

THE <u>CONTRITION</u> OF HAVING HUNG UP ON HIM.

767

The <u>chagrin</u>
over a thoughtless,
hurtful word.

768

The <u>surprise</u> when
someone is unexpectedly
accommodating.

769

THE <u>LONGING</u>
TO BE ASKED
FOR ADVICE.

770

The <u>affectionate</u> <u>sense</u>
of knowing exactly what's
going on in his mind.

771

The <u>horror of realizing</u>
that you could have died in
that close shave just now.

772

The

ENVY

of your thrifty friends who always get
everything cheaper, whereas money just
slips away through your hands.

773

The <u>amazement</u> that
people think you're cheerful
and laid-back.

774

The <u>shame</u> that
you're just faking all
your friendliness.

775

The _sadness_ of returning to a familiar place
one summer evening twenty years later
without meeting anyone from back then.

776

The _infuriation_
over other people's
minor infractions.

777

THE _HOPE_
THAT FATE WILL LEND
A HELPING HAND.

778

The _disappointment_ of not
feeling anything in particular
on the best day of your life.

779

The _gladness_ of having
someone to eat lunch with
in the cafeteria today.

780

THE <u>SELF-LOATHING</u> WHEN YOU'VE SAID *"GREAT BUZZ"* AND *"THINKING OUTSIDE THE BOX"* AGAIN.

781

The profound <u>satisfaction</u> of explaining something and being understood.

782

The

~≋~ 𝔼ℕ𝕍𝕐 ~≋~

of the cell phone yakkers on the train who seem so grounded and probably always get a good night's sleep and can actually do a two-finger whistle.

783

THE <u>RELIEF</u> THAT THE DOCTOR IS LISTENING TO YOU PATIENTLY.

784

The fear of
having to take the exit for
Tombstone one day.

785

The bitterness
of already knowing
what's inside.

786

THE PRIDE IN
YOUR STUDENTS'
SUCCESS.

787

The consternation
when everyone
meekly obeys.

788

The infinite disappointment
of not getting the top present
on your wish list.

789
The <u>longing</u> for
vacation when you look out
the classroom window.

790
THE <u>FEAR</u> THAT DAD'S ABOUT TO SLAM
ON THE BRAKES AND PUNCH THE
DRIVER BEHIND US IN THE FACE.

791
The <u>determination</u>
to give it another try
right away.

792
**THE
<u>CONTEMPT</u> OF PHYSICAL
WEAKNESS.**

793
THE <u>HOPE</u> THAT
THE CAT WILL HOLD
STILL AT THE VET.

THE WRETCHEDNESS at the sight of the girl who was your BFF yesterday playing with her new BFF today.

795

The _desperation_ of
struggling for the right words when
they just refuse to come.

796

THE _HOPE_ THAT
EVERYTHING WILL TURN OUT
OK AFTER ALL.

797

The j_o_y of
sharing all you have
with them.

798

The
⊱⊱**AFFECTION**⊰⊰
at the matter-of-fact way
your wife uses candles and scarves
to give even the crummiest hotel
room a homey feeling.

799

THE INFURIATION OF HAVING TAKEN TOO LITTLE WATER.

800

The fear of possibly running into the new neighbor on the stairs.

801

THE HANKERING FOR AN UPCOMING CHALLENGE.

802

The DISAPPOINTMENT that other people get by just fine without advice and assistance.

803

*The tenderness
you feel for your child
in the school play.*

804

The

EMBARRASSMENT

of seeing your parents in the
audience of the school play with their
faces lit up like Christmas trees.

805

The self-loathing when
you didn't get any real work
done with that extra time.

806

*The rather solitary
confidence that you're a
really good dancer.*

807

The

DISCOMFORT

of walking on a deserted street
at night behind a woman who probably
thinks you're stalking her.

808

The perplexity
as to why they've stopped
saying hi to you.

809

The
infuriation with the DJ
at the wedding.

810

THE LONGING
FOR SOMETHING
UNATTAINABLE.

811

THE HELPLESS EXASPERATION WHEN
THE OTHERS COULDN'T CARE LESS HOW
THIS PROJECT TURNS OUT.

812

The pride of getting to
show off shamelessly in front
of your favorite uncle.

813

The bitterness that you
missed a lifetime opportunity
and didn't even give it a try.

814

The hope
of running into him
by chance.

815

The irritation
over your family's indecisive
weekend day-trip planning.

816

THE **FEAR** OF ONE
DAY ENDING UP LIKE THAT
WOMAN THERE.

817

The

ELATION

of roaring around on your new motorcycle
in great weather and picturing how
cool everyone thinks you are.

818

The fear that
your feet will
never thaw.

819

The pain
of suddenly missing a
deceased loved one.

820

The _self-satisfaction_ of clearly being the only person in the world who never uses those stupid smileys.

821

The <u>happiness</u> of realizing that you actually have no worries at the moment.

822

The _fear_ that this moment will pass much too quickly.

823

The <u>desire</u> to sleep with that total stranger up there, right this moment.

824

THE <u>DISAPPOINTMENT</u> OF NEVER HAVING EXPERIENCED THE "GOOD OLD DAYS."

825

The <u>hope</u> that
inner serenity will come by
itself as you get older.

826

THE <u>GRATITUDE</u> OF FINALLY
GETTING A CLEAR EXPLANATION OF
SOMETHING COMPLICATED.

827

The <u>irritation</u> of
having to explain the
simplest things.

828

The <u>affection</u> toward yourself
for actually crying again at
the end of *Out of Africa*.

829

The <u>remorse</u> at
having been so mean
to him.

830

The gratitude that
you're a girl, when you look at
all those uptight guys.

831

The ambition
to "convert"
gay men.

832

The

Schadenfreude

when dog owners
step in
dog shit.

833

THE SELF-LOATHING
WHEN CHEWING
YOUR NAILS.

834

THE TIMIDITY AS YOU CLIMB THE PLATFORM
FOR THE BUNGEE JUMP YOUR BEST GIRLFRIEND
GAVE YOU A GIFT CERTIFICATE FOR.

835

The

to find some way to praise your
good friends' botched dinner.

836

The relief when
your parents didn't curse
you out after all.

837

THE JOY
OF HITTING THE NAIL
ON THE HEAD.

THE fear OF CONSTANTLY FALLING IN LOVE.

839
THE <u>TRIUMPH</u>
OF HAVING
SHOWN THEM ALL.

840
The old <u>pain</u> of seeing
children cry and remembering
exactly how that was.

841
*The <u>despair</u> when
everything conspires against
you yet again.*

842
The <u>panic</u> that
another seizure could come
at any moment.

843
The <u>indignation</u> that your
little siblings suddenly get to do all the
things you fought so hard for.

844

The helpless _distress_ at the sight
of the teenage son you'd like to help
out of his misery, but can't.

845

THE _REMORSE_ AT
HAVING TURNED DOWN AN
UNBEATABLE OFFER.

846

The _relief_ when
the test comes back
negative.

847

The _longing_
for a day
with no pain.

848

The _gratitude_
that things took a turn for
the better after all.

849

THE _PANIC_ WHEN THE DENTIST SAYS, "YOU MIGHT FEEL A LITTLE PRICK NOW."

850

Anticipation of your grandchildren's visit.

851

Thankfulness for unexpected solace.

852

HUNGRYTIR EDHAVETOP EETHIRSTY.

853

The despair
that you can't change
who you are.

854

THE WORRY

WHETHER THE CAR WILL MAKE

IT TO DISNEY WORLD.

855

The

when your parents embrace
again and don't let go.

856

The anger
at your own
laziness.

857

THE
GRIM RESOLUTION OF
PULLING WEEDS.

858

The _suspense_ before
opening the next door in
the Advent calendar.

859

The _anger_ when
praise you totally earned
isn't forthcoming.

860

The _horror of_
happening upon a vicious
street fight.

861

The _happiness_
of admiring a freshly
painted wall.

862

YOUR ETERNAL

OF FLATTERY, BECAUSE YOU DON'T THINK
THERE'S ANYTHING FLATTERING TO
SAY ABOUT YOU ANYWAY.

863

The <u>indignation</u> at
being called
vain.

864

The <u>astonishment</u> that you
weren't even looking for a partner
for life, and found one after all.

865

The <u>fear</u> of constantly being
outsmarted and never noticing
until it's too late.

866

The dread of being
a spectator in court as an
indictment is read.

867

The

of having a mental blackout
when your son's on *Millionaire*
and uses the phone-a-friend option
for the million-dollar question.

868

The desperate
longing to lose control
just once.

869

THE SHAME OF
BEING THE LAST PERSON
PICKED FOR THE TEAM.

870

The relief that
other people struggle with
their flaws as well.

871

**The envy of
the victims for getting
all the sympathy.**

872

THE WORRY THAT YOU MIGHT
WALK PAST YOUR MOTHER ON THE
STREET WITHOUT NOTICING HER.

873

The loneliness
during the first night
of the stomach flu.

874

THE DISILLUSIONMENT
OF REALIZING THAT'S REALLY
ALL YOU'RE GETTING.

875

THE LONGING TO FIND SOME WAY TO PUT THE BLAME ON OTHER PEOPLE.

876

The hatred of the victims for being morally impeachable.

877

The uneasiness when you realize they're talking about you over there.

878

The hope that more than a photo will remain once she's gone.

879

THE BITTERNESS OVER YOUR BODY'S DETERIORATION.

880

The _shame_ of having long since drifted off, even though she's telling you something important.

881

The _perplexity_ over a vague yearning that just refuses to let go.

882

The _consternation_ when you'd meant everything for the best.

883

The **astonishment** that your friends have such a high opinion of you.

884

The _happiness_ that this chance acquaintanceship turned into a real friendship.

885

THE ANGER AT FATE
FOR MAKING YOU THE MIDDLE
SIBLING OF THREE.

886

THE ANGER WHEN YOUR
COLLEAGUE POKES YOU IN THE RIBS
AGAIN IN THAT PALSY-WALSY WAY.

887

THE ANGER AT YOUR
HUSBAND, WHO FORGOT TO TURN OFF
THE ALARM CLOCK ON SUNDAY.

888

THE ANGER AT PEOPLE
WHO ALWAYS KNOW EXACTLY
WHAT'S BEST FOR YOU.

889

THE ANGER WHEN SOMEONE EXPLAINS
TO YOU FOR THE MILLIONTH TIME THAT IT'S
REALLY PERFECTLY SIMPLE.

890

The _anger_ at the
shit-eating grin of the person
you're talking to.

891

The _anger_ at
the whiny school group
at the theater.

892

The _anger_ at the
sauce stain on your shirt just
before giving your talk.

893

The _anger_ when he
shoves you from behind
again.

894

The _anger_
at asinine slogans
everyone buys into.

896

The

S H A M E

about the fear
that your son could
turn out gay.

897

The <u>thankfulness</u>
that not everything has
gone totally wrong yet.

898

The <u>helplessness</u>
at a cheeky reply from
your teenager.

899

The <u>anticipation</u> of how
Pacquiao is going to totally
kick the other guy's ass.

900

THE HATRED OF
BIG MEN WITH BIG
CARRY-ON BAGS.

901

THE SHAME
OF BEING CAUGHT
FIBBING.

902

THE SHOCK

OF REALIZING THAT YOU LOVE

HER UNCONDITIONALLY.

903

The unexpected sense of
well-being upon entering
an unfamiliar space.

904

The relief at
a certain person's
death.

905

The <u>torment</u> of waiting for Christmas.

906

The <u>affection</u> of realizing how well your friends know you.

907

THE <u>UNCERTAINTY</u> WHETHER YOU DREAMED THAT OR ACTUALLY EXPERIENCED IT.

908

The <u>joy</u> that he really does like me without makeup.

909

The <u>fright</u> at the bottomless depths beneath you when snorkeling on the open sea.

910

The regret at having spontaneously invited to dinner people you have nothing in common with.

911

THE HOPE THAT THIS VOID WITHIN YOU WILL FILL AGAIN.

912

The shock at what a fool you just made of yourself without even noticing it.

913

THE SATISFACTION *OF NOT HAVING GOTTEN OFF THE TREADMILL BEFORE COMPLETING THE ENTIRE WORKOUT.*

914
THE *ANNOYANCE* AT PEOPLE
WHO DON'T WASH THEIR HANDS
IN PUBLIC RESTROOMS.

915
The assurance that
we'll sit together like this
many times yet to come.

916
The *uncontrollable* joy
over the first steps taken
after a long illness.

917
The *impotent rage*
that it had to hit you
of all people.

918
The pride at
having put one over on the
obnoxious colleague.

919

The
DEATH-DEFYING
COURAGE

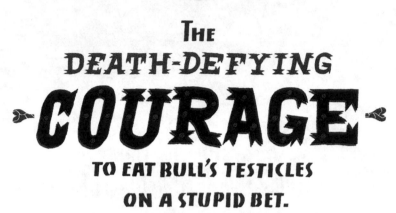

TO EAT BULL'S TESTICLES
ON A STUPID BET.

920

The helplessness
in the face of your
cat's whims.

921

The satisfaction
when they
flatter you.

922

The despair at your
inability to feel
joy anymore.

923
The affection for your mother
as she opens her first e-mail
at the age of seventy-three.

924
The disappointment at a
game that was undeservedly
lost by a hair.

925
The exasperation
at that eternal damned
shyness of yours.

926
THE RELIEF THAT YOU
ACTUALLY DO HAVE MORE OF A
CLUE NOW THAT YOU'RE OLDER.

927
The annoyance
that your parents still treat
you like a child.

928

The spooky

of having exactly
the same dream
as your wife.

929

The <u>anticipation</u>
of a package you
ordered online.

930

THE <u>FEAR</u> THAT YOUR PARENTS
WILL BARTER YOU AWAY
AT THE BAZAAR.

931

The <u>pleasant</u>
<u>surprise</u> of finding
unexpected allies.

932

The thankfulness that this ordeal will be spared you.

933

The trepidation of watching two archenemies tear into each other on a low-life talk show.

934

THE PRIDE AT THE SURPRISING FRIENDLINESS OF YOUNG WAITERS IN COOL BARS.

935

The despair at the fact that this mistake can't be undone.

936

THE POISE WHEN ABOUT TO DO A TASK YOU'RE REALLY GOOD AT.

937

The

DISDAIN

of character flaws you think
you've long since overcome.

938

THE SELF-SATISFACTION
AFTER SKILLFULLY DRIVING
A HARD BARGAIN.

939

THE ASTONISHMENT
AT AN UNEXPECTED
TASTE.

940

The trepidation about
the letter that will
decide everything.

941

The gratification
at the fact that other
couples fight too.

942

THE HELPLESSNESS OF
NOT KNOWING HOW TO
APOLOGIZE TO HIM.

943

The letdown when
no one picks you up
at the airport.

944

The helplessness
of not being able to
stop yawning.

945

THE ANGER
AT FEIGNED
FRIENDLINESS.

947

THE DESPAIR
OF EVER LIVING UP TO
HIS STANDARDS.

948

The hatred of that old
love song that does nothing but
remind you of how he left you.

949

The
happy anticipation
of cleaning house.

950

The disappointment
in the wake of the first
OkCupid date.

951

The hatred
of the parents who never
stood in your way.

952

THE SENSE
THAT YOU'VE SUDDENLY
TURNED INVISIBLE.

953

The _annoyance_ at having talked
everyone's ears off again at the party
because you were so bored.

954

*The gratitude for
small everyday
pleasures.*

955

*The worry
whether you turned
off the burner.*

956

THE DISAPPOINTMENT
WHEN YOUR HUSBAND ISN'T
COMFORTING ENOUGH.

957

THE <u>ELATION</u>
OF HAVING THIS DAY
ALL TO YOURSELF.

958

The

.✦ when you're accused of ✦.
coldheartedness and you suddenly
wonder if there's something to it.

959

THE <u>PRIDE</u> OF
WAKING UP NEXT TO A
TOTAL STRANGER.

960

The <u>infuriation</u>
at bullshit ads that think
you're a sucker.

961

The gl<u>ee</u> of
watching him trying in
vain to keep his cool.

962

The

of suspecting that she
doesn't even like you.

963

The <u>discomfort</u> of
having to share a table with other
people at a restaurant.

964

The <u>relief</u> of asking
your friends for help and
getting good advice.

965

The disappointment
when a phone call
doesn't come.

966

The peaceful
harmony after
you've had a fight.

967

THE HOPE OF
BEING CAUGHT
SHOPLIFTING.

968

The
pride in your own
nitpickiness.

969

THE RELIEF
THAT THEY DIDN'T
LAUGH AT YOU.

970

The <u>sadness</u> that you'll probably never see your new friends again.

971

The <u>insecurity</u> following a dumb little misunderstanding.

972

THE <u>PRIDE</u> IN BUILDING SOMETHING REALLY STURDY AND USEFUL.

973

The

bitterness

at being the only one who wasn't invited.

974

The certainty that
someday the day
will come.

975

THE PRIDE WHEN
EUROPEANS TAKE YOU
FOR A CANADIAN.

976

The emotion when very poor
people invite you home and serve
you all the food in the house.

977

The satisfaction of
discovering the ultimate insider
tip without a travel guide.

978

The fear of
being an adopted
child.

979

The

with the tiniest little creatures,
because you're constantly putting
yourself in their position.

980

The _triumph_ of
living up to your own
demands for once.

981

The gratification of still being able to follow
the liturgy at a Catholic Mass—even
though you've long since left the church.

982

THE **DOUBT** WHETHER
SHE MIGHT BE RIGHT ABOUT
THAT AFTER ALL.

983
The shame of
having achieved a lot but being
unable to really enjoy it.

984
THE WORRY THAT YOU
MIGHT ACTUALLY BE RIGHT ABOUT
THIS SPONTANEOUS DECISION.

985
The annoyance when you
realize how far off base you were
without even realizing it.

986
The shock of
grasping that not everyone
likes you.

987
The serenity of suddenly
realizing that there's no one
else you want to be.

988

The <u>pleasure</u>
of forgiving yourself
a mistake.

989

The

*of drinking cool white wine with
your parents on a summer evening
and not having to say a word.*

990

The <u>relief</u>
of finally putting the
past behind you.

991

The disa<u>ppointment</u> that
another weekend has passed
without meeting anyone.

992

The <u>thrill</u> of suddenly
hearing your native language
in a foreign country.

993

The <u>misgiving</u> that
there might be something
shady about this deal.

994

THE

OF AN UNEXPECTED

WINDFALL.

995

The pleasant
<u>exhaustion</u> after weeping
tears of joy.

996

The anticipation of the year's first ice cream cone.

997

The self-satisfaction of chopping vegetables and feeling like a celebrity chef.

998

The satisfaction of having cut a halfway decent figure at karaoke. Especially on "Total Eclipse of the Heart."

999

THE GLEE OF HAVING COMPLETELY SCREWED UP A TASK YOU RESENTED.

Index

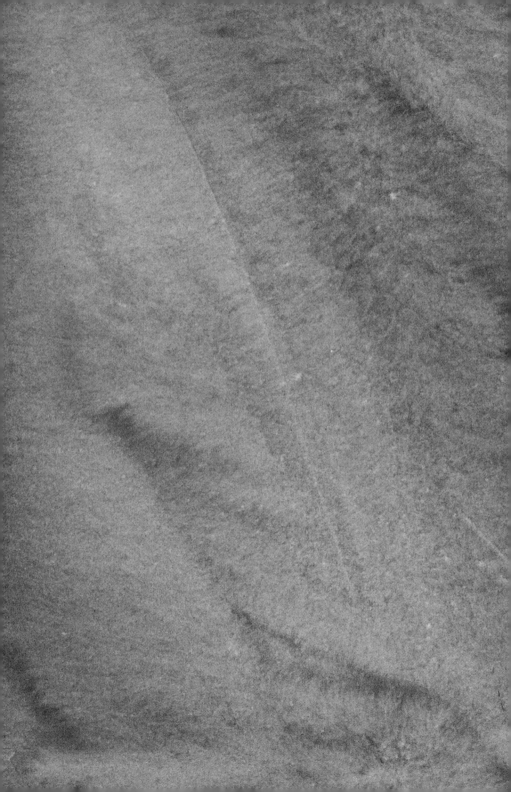